TWENTY-THREE

ESSAYS ON

THE ART OF
LIVING

by
WILFERD A. PETERSON

*including seventeen essays individually pub-
lished in the pages of THIS WEEK Magazine.*

❁ ❁ ❁

INTRODUCTION BY WILLIAM I. NICHOLS

Simon and Schuster, New York
1961

TENTH PRINTING

Library of Congress Catalog Card Number: 61-16562

Manufactured in the United States of America

Introduction

THERE ARE *many arts which make up the Art of Living,
and this little book speaks of a number of them.*

*To the author's selection, I would add one more—the
Art of Inspiration. This is an art—all too rare in these days
—of which Wilferd Peterson is a master. I learned this
fact, dramatically, when we began publication of his essays
for the audience of 14,000,000 families who regularly
receive* This Week Magazine. *Never has a feature drawn
such warm and instant response. And it is in response to
thousands of requests that the essays are now being pub-
lished in permanent form. I hope you will find here, as I
have, a source of wisdom and strength—plus a continuing
reminder that "Man does not live by bread alone"—but
"by faith, by admiration and by sympathy."*

—WILLIAM I. NICHOLS
Editor and Publisher
THIS WEEK Magazine

Contents

❀ ❀ ❀

THE ART OF
GIVING

In gratitude for God's gift of life to us we should share that gift with others. The art of giving encompasses many areas. It is an outgoing, overflowing way of life.

Basically we give what we are. "The thoughts you think," wrote Maeterlinck, "will irradiate you as though you are a transparent vase."

The gifts of *things* are never as precious as the gifts of *thought*.

Emerson said it well: "Rings and jewels are not gifts, but apologies for gifts. The only true gift is a portion of thyself."

We give of ourselves when we give gifts of the heart: love, kindness, joy, understanding, sympathy, tolerance, forgiveness...

We give of ourselves when we give gifts of the mind: ideas, dreams, purposes, ideals, principles, plans, inventions, projects, poetry...

We give of ourselves when we give gifts of the spirit: prayer, vision, beauty, aspiration, peace, faith...

We give of ourselves when we give the gift of time; when we are minute builders of more abundant living for others...

We give of ourselves when we give the gift of words: encouragement, inspiration, guidance...

We should give of ourselves with the radiant warmth of sunshine and the glow of the open fire.

We should give our community a good man.

We should give our home a devoted husband and father.

We should give our country a loyal citizen.

We should give our world a lift toward "that one far-off divine event toward which all creation moves."

The finest gift a man can give to his age and time is the gift of a constructive and creative life. ✹ ✹ ✹

THE ART OF
TRAVELING

WHEN you pack your bags to explore the beauties of your own country or to travel around the world, consider these keys to a happy journey:

Travel lightly. You are not traveling for people to see you!

Travel slowly. Jet planes are for getting places not seeing places; take time to absorb the beauty and inspiration of a mountain or a cathedral.

Travel expectantly. Every place you visit is like a surprise package to be opened. Untie the strings with an expectation of high adventure.

Travel hopefully. "To travel hopefully," wrote Robert Louis Stevenson, "is better than to arrive."

Travel humbly. Visit people and places with reverence and respect for their traditions and ways of life.

Travel courteously. Consideration for your fellow travelers and your hosts will smooth the way through the most difficult days.

Travel gratefully. Show appreciation for the many things

that are being done by others for your enjoyment and comfort.

Travel with an open mind. Leave your prejudices at home.

Travel with curiosity. It is not how far you go, but how deeply you go that mines the gold of experience. Thoreau wrote a big book about tiny Walden Pond.

Travel with imagination. As the Old Spanish proverb puts it: "He who would bring home the wealth of the Indies must carry the wealth of the Indies with him."

Travel fearlessly. Banish worry and timidity; the world and its people belong to you just as you belong to the world.

Travel relaxed. Make up your mind to have a good time. Let go and let God.

Travel patiently. It takes time to understand others, especially when there are barriers of language and custom; keep flexible and adaptable to all situations.

Travel with the spirit of a world citizen. You'll discover that people are basically much the same the world around. Be an ambassador of good will to all people. ❁ ❁ ❁

THE ART OF
MASTERING
FEAR

F EAR is a wild horse that needs a tight rein, for it is both friend and foe, both good and evil, and to live effectively a man must learn to master it . . .

By utilizing the intuitive warning system of fear as a shield against real danger.

By harnessing the energizing power of fear for flight or fight when an emergency strikes.

By using the fear of insecurity, defeat and failure as a lash and spur to high achievement.

By guarding against fear's power to destroy through recalling the ancient legend of the Plague that went to Bagdad to kill five thousand people. Fifty thousand died instead and when the Plague was questioned, it replied: "I killed five thousand as I said I would, the others died of fright!"

By flooding the dark corners of fear and superstition with the bright light of reason and knowledge, thus mapping the unknown, overcoming fancy with fact, dispersing hobgoblins of the imagination and revealing the truth that sets men free.

By accepting the fact that old age and death are natural and inevitable, that to fear them is futile, and that they can best be faced with a calm and quiet mind by ignoring them and gallantly living a day at a time.

By finding inspiration in the words of Cardinal Newman: "Fear not that your life shall come to an end but rather that it shall never have a beginning."

By willingly taking the risk of enriching adventures tinged with danger, knowing that the sheltered and protected life misses much and that as the Bard of Avon expressed it: "Cowards die many times before their deaths; the valiant never taste of death but once."

By facing fear boldly and practicing the precept of Emerson: "Do the thing you fear and the death of fear is certain."

By coming into alignment with the great spiritual laws of the universe and learning that "God has not given us the spirit of fear, but of power and of love and of a sound mind."

By discovering that the mightiest law of all is this: "Perfect love casts out fear."

By beholding the power of faith to work miracles, as expressed in these inspiring words: "Fear knocked at the door. Faith opened it. And lo, there was no one there!"

13

THE ART OF
BEING
YOURSELF

$\mathcal{T}$HE art of being yourself at your best is the art of unfolding your personality into the man you want to be. A famous biologist has said that the possibility of even identical twins being wholly alike is one chance to all of the electrons in the world; each man is a unique individual being.

By the grace of God you are what you are; glory in your selfhood, accept yourself and go on from there.

A good place to begin is by having faith in yourself and your destiny. "Trust yourself," wrote Emerson, "every heart vibrates to that iron string."

Champion the right to be yourself; dare to be different and to set your own pattern; live your own life and follow your own star.

Respect yourself; you have the right to be here and you have important work to do.

Don't stand in your own shadow; get your little self out of the way so your big self can stride forward.

14

Make the most of yourself by fanning the tiny spark of possibility within you into the flame of achievement.

Follow the advice of Socrates: Know Thyself; know your strengths and your weaknesses; your relation to the universe; your potentialities; your spiritual heritage; your aims and purposes; take stock of yourself.

Create the kind of self you will be happy to live with all your life.

Consider the words of the new convert who prayed: "Oh, Lord, help me to reform the world beginning with *me*."

Be gentle with yourself, learn to love yourself, to forgive yourself, for only as we have the right attitude toward our selves can we have the right attitude toward others.

In the relationship of yourself with all of the other selves of the world follow the wise axiom of Shakespeare, who wrote: "To thine own self be true, and it must follow, as the night the day, thou canst not then be false to any man."

15

THE ART OF
LAUGHTER

Meet the challenge of life with the art of laughter ... Take a tip from Will Rogers who observed people with laughter in his eyes and love in his heart and declared: "I never met a man I didn't like."

Learn laughter from little children by thinking their thoughts, dreaming their dreams and playing their games.

Develop a playful attitude toward problems; toss them around; handle them with a light touch.

Practice the advice of the psychiatrist who gives his normal patients this prescription: "Don't take yourself so damned seriously."

Use laughter as a safety valve to keep yourself sane and relaxed. Emerson said it well: "The perception of the Comic is a tie of sympathy with other men, a pledge of sanity. We must learn by laughter as well as by tears and terror."

Remember the old proverb: "A little nonsense now and then is relished by the wisest men."

Consider the power of laughter to prick the balloons of pretense and to deflate stuffed shirts.

Inject laughter into tense situations to save the day; laughter calms tempers and soothes jangled nerves.

Use laughter to set healing vibrations into motion—to fill a room with the sunshine of good cheer.

Guard yourself against the gloomy outlook by recalling the wise statement of Henry Ward Beecher: "A man without mirth is like a wagon without springs...he is jolted disagreeably by every pebble in the road."

Tell the funny story on yourself so that the laugh is on you; always laugh *with* others never *at* them.

Look at the funny side of your difficulties; impersonal contemplation is the secret of laughter and perspective.

Most of all, learn to laugh at yourself; meet each day with a sense of humor.

Laughter is the best medicine for a long and happy life. He who laughs...lasts! ✹ ✹ ✹

AWARENESS

$\mathcal{T}$HOREAU wrote: "Only that day dawns to which we are awake." The art of awareness is the art of learning how to wake up to the eternal miracle of life with its limitless possibilities.

It is rising to the challenge of the stirring old hymn: "Awake my soul, stretch every nerve."

It is developing the deep sensitivity through which you may suffer and know tragedy, and die a little, but through which you will also experience the grandeur of human life.

It is following the philosophy of Albert Schweitzer who teaches "reverence for life," from ants to men; it is developing a sense of oneness with all life.

It is identifying yourself with the hopes, dreams, fears and longings of others, that you may understand them and help them.

It is learning to interpret the thoughts, feelings and moods of others through their words, tones, inflections, facial expressions and movements.

It is keeping mentally alert to all that goes on around you;

it is being curious, observant, imaginative that you may build an ever increasing fund of knowledge of the universe.

It is striving to stretch the range of eye and ear; it is taking time to look and listen and comprehend.

It is searching for beauty everywhere, in a flower, a mountain, a machine, a sonnet and a symphony.

It is knowing wonder, awe and humility in the face of life's unexplained mysteries.

It is discovering the mystic power of the silence and coming to know the secret inner voice of intuition.

It is avoiding blind spots in considering problems and situations; it is striving "to see life steadily and see it whole."

It is enlarging the scope of your life through the expansion of your personality.

It is through a growing awareness that you stock and enrich your memory . . . and as a great philosopher has said: "A man thinks with his memory." ✴ ✴ ✴

THE ART OF
Thinking

$\mathcal{T}$HE art of thinking is the greatest art of all, for "as a man thinketh in his heart, so is he." The thinker knows he is today where his thoughts have taken him and that he is building his future by the quality of the thoughts he thinks.

He recognizes his sovereign control of his own mind and decides what will enter his Mental Kingdom through his sense gateways; he thinks for himself, considers the evidence, seeks the truth and builds his life upon it.

He sets no limitations on the power of thought; he recognizes that big thinking precedes big achievement.

He creates mental pictures of his goals, then works to make those pictures become realities.

He knows that everything starts with an idea and that the creative power of thought is the greatest power in the universe.

He sees with the "single eye" of intense concentration, seeking facts just as a powerful searchlight penetrates the darkness.

He keeps an open mind, observing, analyzing, considering, questioning—looking for the hidden key which will unlock the problem.

He thinks of his mind as a factory and gives it the raw material, the facts and data, from which ideas are fashioned.

He thinks both objectively and subjectively; he gathers mental power both from the world without and the mind within.

He uses the magic power of his subconscious mind, commanding it to come up with ideas while he sleeps; he knows that thought, like a tree, grows night and day.

He studies the laws of cause and effect and strives to work in harmony with them.

He approaches problems both intuitively and logically; he uses the light of his imagination to create and his critical mind to judge; he tests inspiration with logic.

He avoids the one-track mind and sends his mind forth in all directions to expand the range of his mental horizons.

He strives to develop a mature mind without losing the simplicity of childhood.

He creates ideas with humility knowing that behind the idea that he calls his own are the thoughts and efforts of many men.

He realizes that he is at his creative best when he is in tune with the Infinite; when he is open and receptive to the higher powers of mind and spirit.

He exercises his God-given power to choose his own direction and influence his own destiny and he tries to decide wisely and well. ❋ ❋ ❋

THE ART OF
FAiLURE

He who hopes to avoid all failure and misfortune is trying to live in a fairyland; the wise man realistically accepts failures as a part of life and builds a philosophy to meet them and make the most of them.

He lives on the principle of "nothing attempted, nothing gained" and is resolved that if he fails he is going to fail while trying to succeed.

He does not set for himself the impossible ideal of always being successful in everything.

He does the best he can and then with a serene spirit accepts what comes.

He learns from the scientist who said, "At best, research is about 99 percent failure and 1 percent success and the 1 percent is the only thing that counts."

He finds courage in the pages of biography which indicate that our greatest men failed many times. For instance, Louis Pasteur was described as "a scientific Phoenix who arose triumphant from the ashes of his own mistakes."

He recognizes that although he cannot always control what happens to him, he can always control how he responds to his failures.

He observes that the only water that can sink a ship is

water that gets inside of it and so he strives to keep all thoughts of failure out of his mind.

He knows that as long as a man keeps his faith in God and in himself nothing can permanently defeat him.

He knows that when the blows of life knock a man down, the important thing is not to stay down. He develops the quality of bounce, rebounding from defeat as a rubber ball rebounds when you throw it to the floor.

He knows that life has its rhythms, as the ebb and flow of the tide, so he learns "to labor and to wait," giving time a chance to work its miracles.

He uses the lessons of failure to build for the future; his mistakes become red stop lights warning him away from highways that lead to defeat.

He learns to fall forward like a good ball carrier in football . . . to make the most of every failure.

He rises to the challenge of failure as did Mark Twain when he wrote, "A few fly bites cannot stop a spirited horse."

He keeps on keeping on.

He adopts as his talisman the magic words of the ancient seer: "This, too, shall pass away." ✸ ✸ ✸

ADVENTURE

A MAN practices the art of adventure when he heroically faces up to life ... When he says, like Frank Crane: "My soul is a Columbus; and not watery wastes, nor glooming mysteries ... shall send me back, nor make me cry 'Enough!'"

When he has the daring to open doors to new experiences and to step boldly forth to explore strange horizons.

When he is unafraid of new ideas, new theories and new philosophies.

When he has the curiosity to experiment ... to test and try new ways of living and thinking.

When he has the flexibility to adjust and adapt himself to the changing patterns of life.

When he refuses to seek safe places and easy tasks and has, instead, the courage to wrestle with the toughest problems and difficulties.

When he valiantly accepts the challenge of mountain-top tasks and glories in a job well done.

When he has the moral stamina to be steadfast in the

support of those men in whom he has faith and those causes in which he believes.

When he breaks the chain of routine and renews his life through reading new books, traveling to new places, making new friends, taking up new hobbies and adopting new viewpoints.

When he considers life a constant quest for the noblest and best.

When he has the nerve to move out of life's shallows and venture forth into the deep.

When he recognizes that the only ceiling life has is the one he gives it and comes to realize that he is surrounded by infinite possibilities for growth and achievement.

When he keeps his heart young and his expectations high and never allows his dreams to die.

When he concludes that a rut is only another name for a grave and that the only way to stay out of ruts is by living adventurously and staying vitally alive every day of his life.

THE ART OF
SELLING

WHEN everybody sells, goods, services and ideas move faster, and prosperity is achieved.

Selling is not limited to people called salesmen, for we all have something to sell, and that includes *you!*

When everybody sells, we create a mental and emotional climate of friendliness and good will that makes buying a joyous, happy adventure.

Customers are won and held through a multitude of acts and attitudes. Here are some of the things that represent the art of selling at its best:

Courteous words instead of sharp retorts.

Smiles instead of blank looks.

Enthusiasm instead of dullness.

Response instead of indifference.

Warmth instead of coldness.

Understanding instead of the closed mind.

Attention instead of neglect.

Patience instead of irritation.

Sincerity instead of sham.

Consideration instead of annoyance.

Remembering people instead of forgetting them.

Facts instead of arguments.

Creative ideas instead of the humdrum.

Helpfulness instead of hindrance.

Giving instead of getting.

Action instead of delay.

Appreciation instead of apathy.

Everyone selling together blends hearts and minds and spirits, as the musicians in an orchestra harmonize musical tones, to create a mighty symphony of prosperity.

Let's earn more business by deserving the business we have.

Let's roll out the red carpet for the most important person in the world ... the customer.

Let's everybody sell! ❋ ❋ ❋

THE ART OF
happiness

You can't pursue happiness and catch it. Happiness comes upon you unawares while you are helping others. The philosophy of happiness is pointedly expressed in the old Hindu proverb, which reads: "Help thy brother's boat across, and lo! thine own has reached the shore."

Happiness is like perfume—you can't spray it on others without getting some on yourself.

Happiness does not depend upon a full pocketbook, but upon a mind full of rich thoughts and a heart full of rich emotions.

Happiness does not depend upon what happens outside of you but on what happens inside of you; it is measured by the spirit in which you meet the problems of life.

Happiness is a state of mind. Lincoln once said: "We are as happy as we make up our minds to be."

Happiness doesn't come from doing what we like to do

but from liking what we have to do.

Happiness comes from putting our hearts in our work and doing it with joy and enthusiasm.

Happiness does not come from doing easy work but from the afterglow of satisfaction that comes after the achievement of a difficult task that demanded our best.

Happiness grows out of harmonious relationships with others, based on attitudes of good will, tolerance, understanding and love.

Happiness is found in little things: a baby's smile, a letter from a friend, the song of a bird, a light in the window.

Happiness comes from keeping constructively busy; creative hobbies are the keys to happy leisure hours and retirement years.

The master secret of happiness is to meet the challenge of each new day with the serene faith that: "All things work together for good to them that love God." ❀ ❀ ❀

THE ART OF
FRIENDSHIP

*T*HE first step in the art of friendship is to be a friend; then making friends takes care of itself. To be a friend a man should start by being a friend to himself, by being true to his highest and best and by aligning himself with the enduring values of human life that make for growth and progress.

To be a friend a man should strive to be "like the shadow of a great rock in a weary land," to be a source of refuge and strength to those who walk in darkness.

To be a friend a man should believe in the inherent goodness of men and in their potential greatness; he should treat men in a big spirit, expectant of a noble response.

To be a friend a man should strive to lift people up, not cast them down; to encourage, not discourage; to set an example that will be an inspiration to others.

To be a friend a man should be sensitively responsive to the dreams and aims of others and should show sincere appreciation for the contributions others make to the enrichment of his life.

To be a friend a man should practice the companionship of silence and the magic of words that his speech may build and not destroy, help and not hinder.

To be a friend a man should close his eyes to the faults of others and open them to his own.

To be a friend a man should not attempt to reform or reprimand, but should strive only to make others happy if he can.

To be a friend a man should be himself, he should be done with hypocrisy, artificiality and pretense, he should meet and mingle with people in quiet simplicity and humility.

To be a friend a man should be tolerant, he should have an understanding heart and a forgiving nature, knowing that all men stumble now and then, and that he who never made a mistake never accomplished anything.

To be a friend a man should join hands with all people who are working for great principles, great purposes and great causes; he should put his shoulder to the wheel to help achieve common goals.

To be a friend a man should go more than halfway with his fellow men; he should greet others first and not wait to be greeted; he should radiate a spirit of overflowing good will.

To be a friend a man should remember that we are human magnets; that like attracts like, and that what we give we get.

To be a friend a man should recognize that no man knows all the answers, and that he should add each day to his knowledge of how to live the friendly way. ❉ ❉ ❉

31

THE ART OF
PERSONAL EFFICIENCY

To manage others successfully, a man must first manage himself. Personal efficiency is creative self-management. It is not getting ahead of others, but getting ahead of yourself.

It is having the drive to get started on the task at hand. "Life leaps like a geyser," wrote Alexis Carrel, "for those who drill through the rock of inertia."

It is experimenting to find the best, easiest and quickest ways of getting things done.

It is putting first things first, doing one thing at a time and developing the art of intensive concentration.

It is breaking big tasks down into their smaller parts, simplifying the complex, finishing the big job one step at a time.

It is not being a slave to system but making system a slave to you.

It is making notes and letting pencil and paper remember for you.

It is using Kipling's "six honest serving men"—What and

Why and When and How and Who and Where.

It is building the efficient mentality of balance, perception, organization, ability and stamina.

It is seeking the counsel of wise men in person and through their writings and using their wisdom and experience to help you to live efficiently.

It is weaving the cables of constructive habit so that right action will become automatic. In sport and in business good habits mark the champion.

It is having a goal and mapping out a personal program of how to reach it.

It is setting up personal incentives—promising yourself rewards for work completed.

It is guiding your life instead of drifting.

It is organizing your personal life for efficient living in all the important areas: work, play, love and worship.

It is making time live for you by making the most of every minute. ✤ ✤ ✤

THE ART OF
RELAXATiON

MODERN man must learn to break the tensions of daily living or the tensions will break him.

He must learn to bend with the stresses and strains like a tree in the wind. He must develop the resiliency of spirit to spring erect again after the storm has passed.

He first relaxes his mind by thinking thoughts of peace, quietness and tranquility. He mentally pictures the placid pool amidst whispering pines and puts himself in tune with nature's calming mood.

He strives to carry an inner serenity with him so that even amidst a whirl of activity he will not lose his poise. He learns "to cooperate with the inevitable" and he accepts life with faith in the ultimate triumph of right and good.

He relaxes his body by imitating a lazy person—a boy on the beach in the sun—a man in a boat fishing. He takes a tip from the circus clown who says that the way he avoids being injured in his tumbles is by making his body become "like an old rag doll."

He exercises—walks, stretches, works in the garden, plays

golf—knowing that physical tiredness invites relaxation and sleep.

He knows that confusion is one of the chief causes of tension so he organizes his work, puts first things first, does one thing at a time, avoids hurry and develops a spaciousness of mind.

He uses the soothing beauty of great music to calm his nerves.

He observes that the face with a frown marks the tense person, and that the face with a smile is a symbol of relaxation, so he strives to meet life with a sense of humor. He learns not to take himself too seriously and to laugh at himself now and then.

He takes time for meditation. He accepts the wise counsel of Emerson, who wrote: "Place yourself in the middle of the stream of power and wisdom which animates all whom it floats, and you are without effort impelled to truth, to right and a perfect contentment."

He recognizes that relaxed living is a way of life and strives to manage body, mind, heart and spirit as efficiently as he manages his business. ✸ ✸ ✸

Leadership

SIMPLY and plainly defined, a leader is a man who has followers. The leader deserves to have followers. He has earned recognition. Authority alone is no longer enough to command respect.

The leader is a great servant. The Master of Men expressed the ideal of leadership in a democracy when he said, "And whosoever will be chief among you, let him be your servant."

The leader sees things through the eyes of his followers. He puts himself in their shoes and helps them make their dreams come true.

The leader does not say, "Get going!" Instead he says, "Let's go!" and leads the way. He does not walk behind with a whip; he is out in front with a banner.

The leader assumes that his followers are working with him, not for him.

He considers them partners in the work and sees to it that they share in the rewards. He glorifies the team spirit.

The leader duplicates himself in others. He is a man builder. He helps those under him to grow big because he realizes that the more big men an organization has the stronger it will be.

The leader does not hold people down, he lifts them up. He reaches out his hand to help his followers scale the peaks.

The leader has faith in people. He believes in them, trusts them and thus draws out the best in them. He has found that they rise to his high expectations.

The leader uses his heart as well as his head. After he has looked at the facts with his head he lets his heart take a look, too. He is not only a boss—he is also a friend.

The leader is a self-starter. He creates plans and sets them in motion. He is both a man of thought and a man of action—both dreamer and doer.

The leader has a sense of humor. He is not a stuffed shirt. He can laugh at himself. He has a humble spirit.

The leader can be led. He is not interested in having his own way, but in finding the best way. He has an open mind.

The leader keeps his eyes on high goals. He strives to make the efforts of his followers and himself contribute to the enrichment of personality, the achievement of more abundant living for all and the improvement of civilization.

bEiNG

$\mathcal{T}$HE art of being is the assumption that you may possess, this very minute, those qualities of spirit and attitudes of mind that make for radiant living.

It is a philosophy of *being today*, instead of becoming in a tomorrow that never comes.

It is recognizing that courage, joy, serenity, faith, hope and love are immediately available now, and proceeding to open yourself so these qualities can be expressed through you in everyday living.

It is following the maxim of Shakespeare: "Assume a virtue though you have it not"...knowing that the dynamic power of habit can build it into your character.

It is being great now, being forgiving now, being tolerant now, being happy now, being successful now, instead of postponing positive and constructive living to some vague and indefinite future.

It is knowing that when we move into the future it becomes the *now*, and that now is the appointed time!

It is facing the fact that your biggest task is not to get

ahead of others, but to surpass yourself.

It is wasting no time dreaming about the rich life you may live next year, or ten years from now; it is beginning to live at your best right now, today.

It is heeding the wisdom of the ancient Chinese seer who observed: "A journey of a thousand miles begins with a single step," and it is taking that step today.

It is beginning today to be the man you want to be.

It is developing an awareness of the infinite possibilities in each magic moment.

It is enlarging the *now* by pouring into it intense creative energy.

It is immortalizing the present moment that your life may have eternal significance.

It is coming into a full realization that the Master voiced the secret of victorious *being*, when He declared that the Kingdom of God is not afar off, but that it is *within you now!* ❋ ❋ ❋

THE ART OF
READING

To practice the art of reading, develop a hungry, curious, questing mind and then seek your answers in books . . . You open doors when you open books . . . doors that swing wide to unlimited horizons of knowledge, wisdom and inspiration that will enlarge the dimensions of your life . . .

Through books you can live a thousand lives in one. You can discover America with Columbus, stand with Lincoln at Gettysburg, work in the laboratory with Edison and walk the fields with St. Francis . . .

Through books you can encompass in your imagination the full sweep of world history. You can watch the rise and fall of civilizations, the ebb and flow of mighty battles and the changing pattern of life through the ages . . .

Through books you can enrich your spirit with the Psalms, the Beatitudes, the thirteenth chapter of First Corinthians and all the other noble writings that are touched with divine fire . . .

Through books you can know the majesty of great poetry, the wisdom of the philosophers, the findings of the scientists . . .

Through books you can start today where the great thinkers of yesterday left off, because books have immortalized man's knowledge. Thinkers, dead a thousand years, are as alive in their books today as when they walked the earth.

Through books you can orient your life to the world you live in, for books link the past, the present and the future.

Read, then, from the vast storehouse of books at your command!

Read several books at a time, turning from one to the other as your mood changes . . . a biography, a novel, a volume of history, a book about your business.

Read with a red pencil in your hand, underlining the important passages, so you can quickly review the heart of the book.

Read something each day. Discipline yourself to a regular schedule of reading. With only fifteen minutes a day you can read twenty books in a year . . .

Read to increase your knowledge, your background, your awareness, your insight . . .

Read to lead . . . read to grow! ✸ ✸ ✸

THE ART OF
SUCCESS

$\mathcal{T}$HERE are no secrets of success. Success is doing the things you know you should do. Success is not doing the things you know you should not do.

Success is not limited to any one area of your life. It encompasses all of the facets of your relationships: as parent, as wife or husband, as citizen, neighbor, worker and all of the others.

Success is not confined to any one part of your personality but is related to the development of all the parts: body, mind, heart and spirit. It is making the most of your *total self*.

Success is discovering your best talents, skills and abilities and applying them where they will make the most effective contribution to your fellow men. In the words of Longfellow it is "doing what you do well, and doing well whatever you do."

Success is harnessing your heart to a task you love to do. It is falling in love with your work. It demands intense concentration on your chief aim in life. It is focusing the full power of all you are on what you have a burning desire to achieve.

Success is ninety-nine per cent mental attitude. It calls for love, joy, optimism, confidence, serenity, poise, faith, courage, cheerfulness, imagination, initiative, tolerance, honesty, humility, patience and enthusiasm.

Success is not arriving at the summit of a mountain as a final destination. It is a continuing upward spiral of progress. It is perpetual growth.

Success is having the courage to meet failure without being defeated. It is refusing to let present loss interfere with your long-range goal.

Success is accepting the challenge of the difficult. In the inspiring words of Phillips Brooks: "Do not pray for tasks equal to your powers. Pray for powers equal to your tasks. Then the doing of your work shall be no miracle, but you shall be the miracle."

Success is relative and individual and personal. It is your answer to the problem of making your minutes, hours, days, weeks, months and years add up to a great life ☼

Thanksgiving

 $\mathcal{T}$ HE art of thanksgiving is *thanksliving*. It is gratitude in action. It is applying Albert Schweitzer's philosophy: "In gratitude for your own good fortune you must render in return some sacrifice of your life for other life."

It is thanking God for the gift of life by living it triumphantly.

It is thanking God for your talents and abilities by accepting them as obligations to be invested for the common good.

It is thanking God for all that men and women have done for you by doing things for others.

It is thanking God for opportunities by accepting them as a challenge to achievement.

It is thanking God for happiness by striving to make others happy.

It is thanking God for beauty by helping to make the world more beautiful.

It is thanking God for inspiration by trying to be an inspiration to others.

It is thanking God for health and strength by the care and reverence you show your body.

It is thanking God for the creative ideas that enrich life by adding your own creative contributions to human progress.

It is thanking God for each new day by living it to the fullest.

It is thanking God by giving hands, arms, legs and voice to your thankful spirit.

It is adding to your prayers of thanksgiving, acts of *thanksliving.* ✹ ✹ ✹

45

THE ART OF
Achievement

*Y*ou hold in your hand the camel's-hair brush of a painter of Life. You stand before the vast white canvas of Time. The paints are your thoughts, emotions and acts.

You select the colors of your thoughts; drab or bright, weak or strong, good or bad.

You select the colors of your emotions, discordant or harmonious, harsh or quiet, weak or strong.

You select the colors of your acts; cold or warm, fearful or daring, small or big.

Through the power of your creative imagination you catch a vision . . . you dream a dream.

You visualize yourself as the man you want to be.

You see yourself as a triumphant personality striding toward far horizons of constructive accomplishment.

You see yourself as a master servant of the race, ministering to human needs, radiating happiness.

You see yourself as a builder, making a creative contribution to the evolution of modern civilization.

You strive to make the ideal in your mind become a reality on the canvas of Time.

You select and mix the positive colors of heart, mind and spirit into the qualities of effective living: patience, determination, endurance, self-discipline, work, love and faith.

Each moment of your life is a brush stroke in the painting of your growing career.

There are the bold, sweeping strokes of one increasing, dynamic purpose.

There are the lights and shadows that make your life deep and strong.

There are the little touches that add the stamp of character and worth.

The art of achievement is the art of making life—*your life*—a masterpiece. ✸ ✸ ✸

THE ART OF
STAYING
YOUNG

*T*HE art of staying young depends upon staying youthful on the *inside,* in mind, heart and spirit, in defiance of wrinkles and gray hairs on the *outside*. The Fountain of Youth is *within* you!

Staying young is an *inside* matter. Your body grows old, but your body is not you. "We do not count a man's years," wrote Emerson, "until he has nothing else to count."

Stay young by continuing to grow. You do not grow old, you become old by not growing.

Stay young by hanging on to your dreams. A philosopher writes: "There is not much to do but bury a man when the last of his dreams is dead."

Stay young by maintaining a cheerful attitude. Keep this verse from Proverbs in mind: "A merry heart doeth good like medicine, but a broken spirit drieth up the bones."

Stay young by keeping your mind alive and alert. Scientists have found that the ability to think does not decline with advancing age; the only difference may be a slight decrease in the speed of thinking.

Stay young by forcing your mind out of old ruts. Remember that beaten paths are for beaten men. See new places, read new books, try new hobbies. Increase the depth of your life.

Stay young by remaining flexible, adaptable and open-minded. Do not permit your mental arteries to harden.

Stay young by taking inspiration from the young in spirit who remained creatively active all their lives: Goethe completing Faust at 80; Titian painting masterpieces at 98; Toscanini conducting at 85; Justice Holmes writing Supreme Court decisions at 90; Edison busy in his laboratory at 84; Benjamin Franklin helping to frame the American Constitution at 80.

Stay young by keeping constructively busy. Set yourself new goals for achievement.

Stay young by tackling new projects. The man who planted a tree at 90 was a man of vision. Start ideas and plans rolling that will go on long after you are gone.

Stay young by doing good. Work for worthy causes in your city, state, nation and world.

Stay young by keeping your heart young. "If it can be done," wrote the poet, Carl Sandburg, "it is not a bad practice for a man of many years to die with a boy heart."

Stay young by knowing that "they who wait upon the Lord shall renew their strength; they shall mount up with wings as eagles; they shall run, and not be weary, and they shall walk, and not faint." ❀ ❀ ❀

THE ART OF
WORK

WORK brings man to life, sets him in motion. Work is man in action doing things. Nothing happens until people go to work. Work creates the world we live in.

The right attitude toward work multiplies achievement.

The art of work consists of what you think about your work, how you feel about your work, and what you do about your work.

It is abolishing the concept of work as chains and slavery, and seeing it as freedom to create and build and help.

It is striving to find work you can love, a job to which you can harness your heart.

It is idealizing your work, turning a job into a mission, a task into a career.

It is doing your present work so well that it will open doors to new opportunities. Tasks done at a high standard pave the way to bigger things.

It is glorifying your work, putting a halo around your job.

50

It is saying with the poet Henry van Dyke: "This is my work, my blessing, not my doom."

It is discovering the great healing power of work. If you are lonely . . . work! If you are worried or fearful . . . work! If you are discouraged or defeated . . . work! Work is the key to happiness.

It is working with enthusiasm, recognizing with Maxim Gorki that "The game is not only worth the candle, it is worth the whole bonfire."

It is making your work *you*. It is putting the stamp of your unique personality on the work you do. It is pouring your spirit into your task. It is making your work a reflection of your faith, your integrity, your ideals.

It is recognizing that work, not repose, is the *destiny* of man. It is only through work that you can express yourself and make a contribution to human progress.

It is going to your work as you go to worship, with a prayer of thankfulness and the aspiration to serve.

James W. Elliott said it all in nine words: "Work is life and good work is good life." ✹ ✹ ✹

THE ART OF
LiVING
FOREVER

No man stands alone. Through all the centuries of recorded time, men have set into motion influences that affect your life today. . . .

You are the heir of the ages. Men reaching for the stars have created for you a world of wonder and challenge. . . .

Living in you now are the ideals of the ragged soldiers of Valley Forge, the gallant Pilgrims, the daring explorers and pioneers, the fighters for freedom through all history. . . .

On a more intimate note, your mother, father, teacher, clergyman, friend have built their influences into your character. . . .

More enduring than skyscrapers, bridges, cathedrals, and other material symbols of man's achievement are the invisible monuments of wisdom, inspiration and example erected in the hearts and minds of men. . . .

Example has immortal momentum. It has been truly said that a boy does not have to be shown a mark on the wall to measure up to, when there is a man around about the size he wants to be. . . .

Mentor Graham, teacher of Lincoln, is forgotten, but his influence lives forever in the Man for the Ages....

Ideas move through time and space changing the world, making all things new, from the discovery of fire and the invention of the wheel to the development of atomic power....

Words are charged with everlasting power. The radiant words of the Sermon on the Mount light the spirits of each generation. The axioms of the great inspire men to "rise on steppingstones of their dead selves to higher things." Simple words expressing courage, faith and love have immortal significance in the lives of millions....

Your example, your words, your ideas, your ideals can also be projected into the future to live forever in the lives of others....

As you help men to grow, as you work for peace, understanding and good will, your influence will merge, with the good influences of men of every age, into the eternal golden stream of God's goodness....

As you throw the weight of your influence on the side of the good, the true and the beautiful, your life will achieve an endless splendor. It will go on in others, bigger, finer, nobler than you ever dared to be. ❀ ❀ ❀

About the Author

WILFERD A. PETERSON, *a writer and an editor, was born in Whitehall, Michigan. He is a long-time resident of Grand Rapids, where he is vice president and creative director for the advertising firm The Jaqua Company.*

LONG-PLAYING RCA RECORD: The Gold Album of Inspiration presents twelve of the Art of Living essays, selected and recorded with his comments by William I. Nichols, Editor and Publisher of *This Week* Magazine. This 33⅓ RCA high-fidelity 12-inch LP record and its beautiful jacket were produced by and may be ordered from:

Edward M. Miller and Associates, Inc.
518 McKay Tower, Grand Rapids 2, Michigan

Price $6.00 each, shipping charges prepaid. Quantity prices on request.